CASTLES

by Michèle Dufresne

Pioneer Valley Educational Press, Inc.

Here is a **castle**.
Long ago, people lived
in castles to be safe.

There are big **walls**
around this castle.
The walls helped keep
people safe.

4

5

There is a **moat**
around this castle.
The moat helped
keep people safe.

There is a **lake** around this castle. The lake helped keep people safe.

There are big towers
on this castle.
The big towers
helped keep people safe.

There are little **windows** on this castle.
The little windows helped keep people safe.

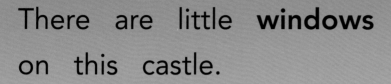

13

Long ago, people
lived in castles
to be safe.

CASTLES

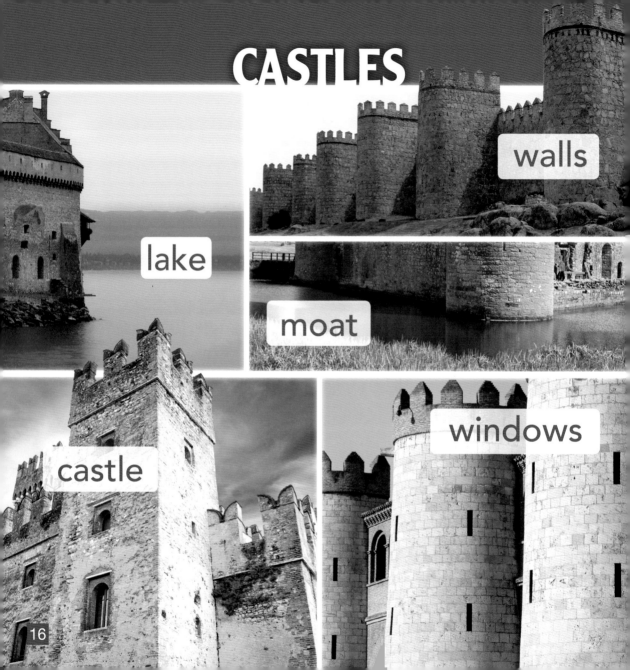

walls

lake

moat

castle

windows